V&R unipress

Gunnar Hering Lectures

Volume 1

Edited by
Maria A. Stassinopoulou

The volumes of this series are peer-reviewed.

Dimitris Stamatopoulos

The Eastern Question or Balkan Nationalism(s)

Balkan History Reconsidered

V&R unipress
Vienna University Press

Bibliographic information published by the Deutsche Nationalbibliothek
The Deutsche Nationalbibliothek lists this publication in the Deutsche
Nationalbibliografie; detailed bibliographic data are available online:
http://dnb.d-nb.de.
ISSN 2625-7092
ISBN 978-3-8471-0830-6

**Publications of Vienna University Press
are published by V&R unipress GmbH.**

Sponsored by the Austrian Society of Modern Greek Studies, the Department for
Cultural Affairs of the City of Vienna (MA 7), the Department of Byzantine and
Modern Greek Studies and the Faculty of Historical and Cultural Studies
at the University of Vienna.

Cover image: The cover image is based on a photograph of the sculpture by
Joannis Avramidis "Mittlere Sechsfigurengruppe", 1980, Bronze, 110 cm,
from the estate of the artist, photograph by Atelier Neumann, Vienna,
courtesy of Julia Frank-Avramidis.
Printed in Germany.
Printed and bound by CPI books GmbH, Birkstraße 10, 25917 Leck, Germany.

Printed on aging-resistant paper.

Gunnar Hering Lectures
General Editor's Introduction

It is with great pleasure that I write the general editor's introduction to the first volume in the short monograph series Gunnar Hering Lectures. The books are based on yearly lectures that take place in spring at the Department of Byzantine and Modern Greek Studies of the University of Vienna. Both the lectures program and the book series are named after the first professor of the Chair of Modern Greek Studies founded in 1982, Gunnar Hering (Dresden 1934–Vienna 1994), a scholar of general and East European history and a specialist in Early Modern and Modern history of the Balkans, in particular of Greece and Bulgaria.

The speakers of the lecture program are encouraged to plan their talk having in mind one of the central characteristics of Modern Greek Studies in Vienna both in teaching and research, as established by Hering and practiced to this day. That is, the talks should not be confined to the borders of Area Studies but rather should be strongly embedded in the wider geographical and conceptual framework of historical thought on Europe and even in the global dimension. We also invite our guests to spend a week at the Special Library of the Department, which houses one of the most substantial collections of books and other media on Modern Greece, and to work in the renowned research landscape of Vienna with its particular relevance to South Eastern Europe. The lectures program was initiated by Dimitris Kousouris and Maria A. Stassinopoulou in 2016. It has been made possible through the welcoming and positive resonance among our colleagues both at the University of Vienna and internationally and the financial support of the Faculty of Historical and Cultural Studies of the University of Vienna and the City of Vienna and its Department for Cultural Affairs (MA 7), to whom we express our most sincere appreciation.

The first book is devoted, as was the initial lecture, to a subject central to Hering's own research: comparative political history of South Eastern Europe. Dimitris Stamatopoulos, professor of Balkan and Late Ottoman History at the Department of Balkan, Slavic and Oriental Studies at the University of Macedonia in Thessaloniki, gladly accepted our invitation to be the first speaker and then the first author of the series. He chose as his topic nationalisms and revolutions, a subject which Hering also researched, in particular political parties and nation-building in the emerging states of the area in the nineteenth and early twentieth century. Olga Katsiardi-Hering was the respondent for this first lecture; once more we would like to express our gratitude for her enthusiastic reaction to our project and her lively and rich participation during the lecture and beyond.

Vienna University Press V&R welcomed the proposition to publish the lectures in this format. Thanks are due to the Vienna University Press V&R committee of the University of Vienna, who accepted the new series in their program and to Oliver Kätsch, who helped us through the early steps from first idea to realization. Stephen Cashmore cast his expert proof-reading eye over the text, and Anke Moseberg applied her talents to the layout and printing.

As the general editor of the series I am indebted to them all.

Maria A. Stassinopoulou
Vienna, May 2018

Preface of the author

This essay is based on a lecture presented in 2016 at the University of Vienna to inaugurate a series of yearly lectures dedicated to Gunnar Hering, a historian whose work marked modern Greek history and historiography on Modern Greece and Southeastern Europe.[1] In particular, his work on the Ecumenical Patriarchate during the time of Cyril Lucaris[2] was a model for my own dissertation[3] as it was the only monograph that also took into consideration the political–diplomatic relations of the Great Powers with this religious institution. Although my

1 I am really grateful to the anonymous reviewer for the constructive comments I received as well as to Professor Maria Stassinopoulou and the Department of Byzantine and Modern Greek Studies of the University of Vienna for the great honor to call me as first speaker in the series of Gunnar Hering lectures. Professor Stassinopoulou significantly contributed to the improvement of the final version of my presentation. But mostly I would like to thank Professor Olga Katsiardi-Hering who accompanied me on this journey not only with her fruitful and supportive comments when I had delivered the lecture in April of 2016 but also with a continuous and reflective discussion on many crucial aspects of the Balkan and Late Ottoman History. I had also the opportunity to elaborate this presentation in the receptive settings of the Leibniz Institute of European History at Mainz as well as of the Program in Hellenic Studies at Princeton University which offered me hospitality once more for accomplishing my research project. I am thankful to the leaders of both. I have tried to retain the original character of a lecture in this essay, while at the same time providing a suitable text for the reader.
2 Gunnar Hering, *Ökumenisches Patriarchat und europäische Politik, 1620–1638*, Wiesbaden: F. Steiner, 1968.
3 Dimitris Stamatopoulos, *Μεταρρύθμιση και Εκκοσμίκευση: προς μια ανασύνθεση της Ιστορίας του Οικουμενικού Πατριαρχείου τον 19ο αιώνα* [*Reform and Secularization: Towards a Reconstruction of the History of the Ecumenical Patriarchate in the 19th Century*], Athens: Alexandria Publications, 2003.

PhD aimed at highlighting the political competition between various interest groups inside the Patriarchate in the nineteenth century, the interpretative approach was based on the relationship between these groups mainly with foreign embassies—as Hering had suggested for the seventeenth century. Presenting the first lecture in this series was thus a double honor for me and I hope my essay will provide food for thought on issues that most certainly preoccupied him too.

Introduction

The last recapture of the Septinsular Republic by French troops after the signing of the Treaty of Tilsit in July 1807 triggered a series of revolutionary actions in the Greek peninsula, just as had happened ten years before, in 1797.

As is well known, Ali Paşa, who had been appointed as Beylerbey of Rumeli in 1803, succeeded in 1807 in appointing his two sons, Muhtar Paşa and Veli Paşa respectively commanders at Trikala (Tirhala) in Thessaly and Tripoli (Tripoliçe) in the Peloponnese.[4] The total domination of Ali Paşa, along with the usual ensuing expropriation of large ownerships of his opponents and redeployment of armatolikia (αρματολίκια) in favor of factions controlled by him directly, caused reactions from the local elites.

---

[4] Dimitris Stamatopoulos, "Constantinople in the Peloponnese: The Case of the Dragoman of the Morea (Tercüman Bey) Georgios Wallerianos", in A. Anastasopoulos, E. Kolovos (eds.), *Ottoman Rule and the Balkans, 1760–1850,* Rethymnon: University of Crete 2007, pp. 149–164.

Indeed, in 1808 two rebellions took place in Thessaly and in the Peloponnese, which were activated by the French presence in the Ionian Islands, but which took ideological and political reference to the recently exploded Serbian Revolution, and had the political goal of overturning the hegemony of Ali Paşa in the Southern Balkan peninsula.

Before we go further, two great similarities between these rebellions with the Serbian one should be identified at this point. Firstly: neither of them sought to turn against Ottoman rule but against the "corrupt" management of Ali Paşa's sons. They were seeking to establish the Ottoman legitimacy and a balanced co-existence between the Christian and the Muslim population. Certainly this basic characteristic of the Serbian Revolution, that is the fact that it did not immediately emerge as nationalist but as restoring Ottoman legitimacy (something that Milos Obrenović would exploit politically in its second phase), could also be traced to the Romanian peasant uprising in Transylvania against the boyar landowners in the winter of 1784–85 under the leadership of the Romanian peasants Vasile Horea and Ioan Closça.[5]

---

[5] The peasant leader, Horea, would claim that he was acting in the name of Emperor Joseph—which, of course, was untrue. The revolutionary demands, as conveyed to the nobles by Carol Brüneck, were: "In the name of the aforementioned leader, known as Horea, and his simpleton followers, the demands are: 1. That the committee of nobles and all owners take an oath on the cross with all their offspring; 2. That there are no longer nobles and that anyone can find a good job from which to earn a livelihood; 3. That the noble-owners abandon their aristocratic holdings forever; 4. That they too pay taxes like all other taxed citizens; 5. That the fields of the nobles be shared among the ordinary people in accordance with the imperial decree that follows; 6. If His Excellency and the Honourable Council of Nobles with their noble landowners accept all the above, I pledge peace, in whose name

Secondly, as in the Serbian case where "the status in statu" autonomy of Osman Pazvantoğlu of Vidin was defining for the direction of the rebellion, so in the case of the rebellions in Thessaly and the Peloponnese the separatist mutinies of Ali Paşa of Ioannina played a decisive role. Of course, the outcome was different; Pazvantoğlu's involvement strengthened the revolutionary mutiny in the sancak of Belgrade,[6] while Ali Paşa's sons managed to suppress the revolts in the very core of Greek lands, quickly and efficiently.

But these similarities should not divert attention from the most crucial difference of the rebellion that took place in the Peloponnese. The cooperation and approach of Christian and Muslim notables, which took place under the French auspices, resulted in discussions that, according to some researchers, could have led to the writing of a code of laws between the two sides. Unfortunately, the text of this final agreement has not yet been

I ask for white flags to be hoisted on high flagpoles and flown on the city's perimeter and at other ponts", *Obiective Programatice. Ultimatul Ţăranilor* [Programmatic Objectives. Ultimatum to the Agrarians], 11 November 1784, in *1848 La Români o Istorie in Date şi Mărturii* [*1848 among the Romanians: a History in Documents and Testimonies*], vol. I, Bucarest: Editura Ştiinţifică şi Enciclopedică 1982, 4–5. Such intense class divisions did not exist in the Belgrade paşalık; nevertheless the invocation of the class differentiation was always an effective revolutionary method. It is perhaps worth adding that the same model of resurgence was followed also by Tudor Vladimirescu in January of 1821 when he proclaimed that the rebels turn against not the Sultan but the authoritarian regime of the Phanariotes and the Boyars; see E. D. Tappe, "The 1821 Revolution in the Romanian Principalities" in R. Clogg (ed.), *The Greek Struggle for Independence*, London: Macmillan 1973, pp. 134–55.

[6] Rossitsa Gradeva, "Osman Pazvantoğlu of Vidin: Between Old and New", *Princeton Papers: Interdisciplinary Journal of Middle Eastern Studies*, XIII (2005) 115–161.

found, but it is certain that the two sides agreed to a joint-state option after the removal of Veli Paşa; a government equally represented by Muslims and Christians (twelve of each). However, this state partnership seems to have acquired an ideological background, since, according to the memoirs of Kolokotronis, the two sides agreed on a joint flag, which would depict the cross along with the crescent. According to Kolokotronis:

> Our flag would have the moon on the one side and the cross on the other [...].[7] If we would conquer the Peloponnese, we would give a report to the Sultan, saying that we had not rebelled against him, but against Veli Paşa – that was the plan.[8]

Still, the maximum goal that the revolutionaries-to-be had raised was autonomy from the Sublime Porte, based by the Serbian model, as mentioned above.

The two French occupations of the Ionian Islands, as well as Napoleon's invasion of Egypt, prepared the way for the destabilization of Ottoman acquisitions in the Balkans and the eruption of two uprisings at the peninsula's opposite ends—at the northern border with the Habsburg dynasty and in the south, which had recently been occupied from the Venetians. The revolts did not begin as such but did end as national, and supposedly were influenced by representatives of the European Enlightenment. This quickly led scholars of Balkan history

---

[7] It is not clear if Kolokotronis meant that the symbols would co-exist in a single representation, or be on different sides of the flag.

[8] Theodoros Kolokotronis, Διήγησις Συμβάντων της Ελληνικής φυλής από το 1770 έως το 1836, [Narration of the events of the Greek nation from 1770 to 1836], Athens: H. Nikolaidou Filadelfeos Publications 1846, 38.

to draw a link to the French Revolution[9] even though it was more likely the result of the Napoleonic Wars rather than the Revolution itself. And the question, therefore, is whether this interplay between the revolts in the Ottoman Balkans and what happened in Western Europe is limited to the influence of 1789 on the early nineteenth-century uprisings in Greece and Serbia, or whether the model can be extended to relate the development of other national movements to the great revolutionary events that took place in Paris during the remainder of the nineteenth century.

A wise man once observed that every capital city is identified with different things. Paris, for instance, is identified with revolutions. In a way, what is written here is nothing but an attempt to delve deeper into the mass emergence of revolutionary uprisings in the heart of continental Europe—even though this process was touched off by the Anglo-Saxon world and culminated with the Communist revolutions in Eurasia—as this occurred in Balkan regions which still, at the time, were in the embrace of the Ottoman and Austrian empires. The eruption of revolutions across Europe seemed to move in the opposite direction of how Hegel had imagined the flow of world history: instead of moving from East to West, with its spirit finally embodied by the Prussian state, it moved from West to East in the wake of Europe's rapid industrialization. Revolution seemed to herald the urbanization of the feudal societies and, one

---

[9] See for example, Paschalis Kitromilidis, *Η Γαλλική Επανάσταση και η Νοτιοανατολική Ευρώπη* [*The French Revolution and Southeastern Europe*], Athens: Diatton Publishing House, 1990, and Dušan T. Bataković, "Balkan-Style French Revolution? The 1804 Serbian Revolution in European Perspective", *Balkanica* XXXVI (2005), 114–128.

might say, this was a self-fulfilling prophecy even in the cases of Russian and Chinese revolutions, albeit with the creation of a massive bureaucracy. Nonetheless, France continued to alter the conditions giving shape to a modern bourgeois state.

Much ink has been spent explaining why Paris persists with revolutions. The likeliest reason, of course, is that the 1789 Revolution did not seal the political and social hegemony of the bourgeoisie as definitively as the English Civil War and Glorious Revolution in the seventeenth century in England did. And before this hegemony could be completed with the Paris revolutions of 1830 and 1848, an unforeseen element emerged on the world stage that forced an alliance of the bourgeoisie with the conservative landowners. But this was not the sole reason: revolution was also steeped in myth as 1789 became the founding moment of modernity. Efforts of the "reactionaries" to dispel this myth had the opposite effect of fanning it. Thus if 1789 marks the rise of civic society in Europe, then 1848 marks the moment the myth was appropriated by the proletariat. But then something interesting happened to European history: the same revolutionary event marked the divergence of the old industrialized nation-states of Western Europe from Central and Eastern Europe. In Western Europe, labor movements fighting social inequality appeared to try to internally resolve the contradictions of urban society while somehow simultaneously reinforcing the social cohesion of aggressively colonial nations where the recession felt by the working classes was softened by the influx of wealth from the colonies. England was the example the others emulated. But in Central and Eastern Europe, Italian and German unification and the simmering crises of the sprawling Ottoman, Habsburg, and post-Crimean War Romanov empires established 1848 as the springboard for a wave of national uprisings that also had a direct impact on the Balkans.

A century after the 1789 French Revolution, Paris experienced a new uprising. It would appear as if the Jacobins were exacting their revenge, yet what is most important is that this emerged from defeat abroad; if the French Revolution created the momentum for Napoleon to crush the Austrians and Prussians at Austerlitz and Jena, and if the English revolutions could take place after the defeat of the Spanish Armada and the security provided by the English Channel, then 1871 will create a new model of revolutionary process triggered by external intervention and military defeat. Russia's defeat by Japan in 1905 and by Germany in 1917, as well as China's defeat by Japan in 1937, replicate this model but on a much larger scale than 1871 Paris: the defeats in these larger cases created the dynamic for a revolution-driven internal restructuring of states that occupy entire continents.

We thus reach the following conclusion that is the springboard for this essay: that the end of the long nineteenth century will be the inverse of its beginning. The century began with a revolution that would trigger two decades of armed conflicts, and it ended with a Great War which, in turn, would set off a revolution that tries to complete the principles on which the French Revolution was founded, especially that of equality.

The three and one paradigms

But how can an examination of revolution related to war offer a new look or interpretation of Balkan history? To date we have seen two basic narratives for revolutionary events in the Balkans from the eighteenth through the twentieth century. One narrative is known as the "Eastern Question." It is the description of the colonial/imperial activity of the Great Powers rolling the dice on the fate of the ailing Ottoman Empire by fomenting nationalist movements, manipulating political elites, while striving to maintain the balance of power between them before embarking on a new war aimed at improving their position on the global chessboard. In the narrative of the "Eastern Question," the protagonist is the West (including in this case Russia and the Habsburg Empire). In reality, this historiographical paradigm corresponds with the classic Orientalist phase of Western colonialism, when the East, and specifically the Ottoman East, looms as an instrument of the superiority of a technologically, culturally, and militarily advanced "Rational West."[10] The exact correlation of the powerful

---

[10] Edouard Driault, *La Question d'Orient depuis ses origines jusqu'a nos jours*, Paris: Félix Alcan 1898, p. 2. It is impressive that until today the use of term has survived even in the work of writers who take its Orientalist origins into consideration, see for example the introduction in Lucien J. Frary and Mara Kozelsky, *Russian-Ottoman borderlands: The Eastern question reconsidered*, Madison, Wisconsin: The University of Wisconsin Press, 2014. The "reconsideration" looks to be more a relegitimization of the concept than a critical transcendence of its past ideological uses. Another way to criticize the latter is to mention multiple Eastern Questions like Mark Mazower (*The Balkans: A Short History*, New York: The New Library 2000, 85–109) or Eliana Augusti

presence of the Great Powers in the eastern Mediterranean is the extensive crisis of the Ottoman Empire, "the Sick Man of Europe," who could not adapt to the spirit of the new times. A dinosaur of a bygone age that had to be extinguished.[11] We could notice that the term "Eastern Question" had dominated in the period since the end of the Crimean War to the outbreak of the Eastern Crisis. However, the classic definition of its content was given by Edward Driault at the end of the nineteenth century:

> La retraite de l'Islam en Europe et en Asie, de part et d'autre du Bosphore et des Dardanelles, donna naissance à la question d'Orient. Son histoire est proprement l'histoire des progrès des nations voisines en détriment des peuples musulmanes.

But this prevalent narrative was challenged in the late nineteenth and early twentieth century by a different one that came to dominate the post-WWI period: the history of the emergence of national movements. During the Ottoman (or Austrian) conquest, the Balkan peoples had

---

(*Questioni d'Oriente. Europa e Impero ottomano nel Diritto internazionale dell'Ottocento*, Napoli; Roma: Edizioni scientifiche italiane, 2013). However, the normalization of a narrative on unsuspecting Great Powers and irredentist Balkan National States could not explain the differentiation of the two different paradigms in the historiography of the nineteenth and twentieth centuries.

[11] In one sense Frederick F. Anscombe, "The Balkan Revolutionary Age", *The Journal of Modern History*, 84:3, September 2012, pp. 572–606 reproduces the old paradigm's insistence of the failed endeavors of the Empire to reform itself. The reflective and contradictory results of the first reforms in the Ottoman Empire must not been neglected. On the contrary, they must be connected with corresponding developments in the West not for confirming the interventional role of the Great Powers but for tracing the influence of the internal splits of the West in the level of social transformation, and also in the level of colonial antagonism.

slipped into centuries of slumber. The French Revolution and the Enlightenment instigated their awakening and promoted them to claim what the West had already achieved: a state with a civil constitution which, above all, safeguarded property individual rights (something unheard of in the Ottoman East until 1858). Whereas in the first narrative the protagonists were the Great Western Powers and Russia, in this new narrative of "ethnocentric" historiography—using the term here broadly with regards to Balkan historiography, from Stavrianos[12] to Jelavić[13] on—the spotlight was taken by the states of the Balkan East, their resistance to the Ottoman conquest, their movements, their uprisings, their revolts, their state-, and nation-building. The Balkan national historiographies might be already constructed in the nineteenth century, but their re-contextualization in a new category of "Balkan nationalisms" realigned them with the new phase of Western colonialism. This pros-pect does not abandon the Orientalist nature of the "Eastern Question" paradigm but completes it with the Orientalist perspective of the peoples previously subjugated to Ottoman authority. And that explains the "co-existence" of the two paradigms at the turn from the nineteenth to the twentieth centuries: the continuous retreat of the use of Eastern Question did not signify a pure split with the discourses on the Balkans. On the contrary, the latter emerged through the broken mirrors of the former.

If the use of the term "Eastern Question" dominated from the Crimean War to the Eastern Crisis, as noted

---

[12] Leften Stavros Stavrianos, *The Balkans Since 1453*, New York: Rinehart, 1958.
[13] Barbara Jelavich, *History of the Balkans*, vol.2, Cambridge-New York: Cambridge University Press, 1983.

above, a series of works which included the word "Balkans" in their title appeared especially at the end of the nineteenth and beginning of the twentieth century—probably the most important of all that of William Miller.[14] But it is extremely interesting that one of the first systematic narrations of the development of the Balkan national movements, the work of J. A. R. Marriot,[15] had been formulated in the interior of the "old" Eastern Question paradigm where actually his narrative on the diplomacy of the "Eastern Question" has been combined with that of the establishment of the Balkan nation-states. But something like this could have taken place only after the end of this process at the beginning of the twentieth century and especially after the end of the First World War. The Greek case is similar in that the first attempts of writing a kind of Balkan history were introduced by a Byzantinist, Konstantinos Amantos in his Οι Βόρειοι γείτονες της Ελλάδας [*The Northern Neighbors of Greece*], Athens, 1922, exactly after the end of the irredentist program of Megali Idea. On the other hand, the most complete Balkan diplomatic history of the twentieth century was also written by a former Byzantinist and specialist in Medieval Serbia, Michail Th. Laskaris, who occupied the position of the History of the Peoples of the Balkan Peninsula (the Mount Aimos Peninsula in the Greek denomination) at the Aristotle University of Thessaloniki a year after Amantos became Professor of Byzantine History in Athens in 1926. But the title of his work was: *The Eastern Question (1800–1923)*, which was

---

[14] William Miller, *The Balkans. Roumania, Bulgaria, Servia, and Montenegro,* New York: G. P. Putnam's sons, 1896.

[15] J. A. R. Marriot, *The Eastern Question. An Historical Study in European Diplomacy,* Oxford: Clarendon Press, 1918.

published in two issues in 1948 and 1955, when the paradigm of the Eastern Question had already collapsed. Amantos, following the line of Miller's work, would influence the intellectual quests of Leften Stavrianos, while at the same time Laskaris, the most solid Slavic Studies scholar of Greece in the inter- and post- war period, would be captive of an old nineteenth-century narration.

One of the basic characteristics of Balkan nationalisms was the effort to gain recognition from the West. In Balkan historiographies, this translates as an attempt to distance themselves from the negative semantic conno-tation of the East. The Ottoman past must not only be disavowed, but must also be shown as being responsible for the region's cultural, economic, and social development. But while the anti-colonial stance of national liberation movements outside Europe led to a critical approach of the Orientalist perspective, in the case of the Balkan national movements there was what we might call a positive stance towards Orientalist stereotypes which were only shaken after the end of the Cold War. Characteristically, publication of Franz Fanon's classic text *Les Damnés de la Terre* (1961) is separated by roughly 30–35 years from the works of three Balkan women—and this may not be accidental—who for the first time questioned the issue of the Orientalist invention of the meaning of the Balkans: Skopetea,[16] Todorova,[17] and Bakić-Heyden.[18]

---

[16] Elli Skopetea, *Η δύση της Ανατολής: εικόνες από το τέλος της Οθωμανικής Αυτοκρατορίας* [*Orient's West/: Images of the End of the Ottoman Empire*], Athens: Gnosi, 1992.

[17] Maria Todorova, *Imagining the Balkans*, Oxford; New York: Oxford University Press, 2009 [¹1997].

[18] Milica Bakić-Hayden, "Nesting Orientalisms: The Case of the Former Yugoslavia", *Slavic Review* 54, Winter 1995, p. 917–31.

These two historiographical examples, which emerged during different phases of Western colonialism—the former during its waxing, the latter during its waning, the former during its classical period, the latter during what we might call the neo-colonialism period—can be synchronized in their acceptance of the model of the Ottoman Empire's decline. The prerequisite for the rise of national movements became the extended crisis of the Ottoman state from the seventeenth century forward— what Halil Inalcik, the famous Turkish historian, called "decline of the Ottoman classical age."

In the wake of the Cold War's end, a new historiographical paradigm appears to take shape. Let us call it the "Empire's paradigm": it did not highlight just the imperial Ottoman past, but also a tendency to rewrite European history not only as a history of the shaping of national states but as two zones of imperial states— colonial and continental. Balkan history was significantly renewed through this perspective, because rather than being interpreted as a fixed cultural and historical entity, it was approached as a border; not as a border between West and East, as suggested by the Eastern Question paradigm, but as the border where the three great continental empires of eastern Europe—the Ottoman, the Habsburg, and the Russian—met and clashed.

The imperial past was linked to the value system of a multicultural society such as the one that showed strong signs of emerging from the collapse of state socialism. Specifically, in the case of the Ottoman Empire, the "peaceful" coexistence of peoples who would later clash violently in order to share its garments would seem like the discovery of a world erased by the era of nationalisms.

However, such an approach has evident limitations in the sense that it often leads to an idealization of aspects of the Ottoman Empire and the orientalist-inspired denouncement of the bad nationalisms that dismantled it (Arnold Toynbee's "The Western Question" could be characterized as an ancestor of this new kind of orientalist discourse).

Naturally, such an analysis would insist not only on a critical handling of the Balkan national discourses and thus the corresponding national movements (the historiographical example of Balkan nationalisms), but also on disputing the model of decline (the historiographical paradigm of the Eastern Question). Indeed, a series of prominent Ottomanists, starting with Suraiya Faroqhi, raised the issue of the interpretation of the Ottoman Empire as an early modern state and thus not so different from those that emerged in Western Europe during the early Ottoman centuries. Even though such an approach remains to be elaborated, given that the Ottoman Empire's rivals accelerated at such a rate that it could not follow them, it broadened the horizons of historical research mainly because, for the first time, and even if indirectly, they tried to compare the empire as well as the entire Ottoman Balkan world with what we schematically call "the West."[19]

---

[19] In the same way, the Confessionalization paradigm as reformulated in the Ottoman imperial context could be also fruitful, historicizing the role of the religion in the emerging of the millet system during the eighteenth and nineteenth centuries. However, although the influence of the interreligious connections with the West (especially during the period of the Religious Wars or the age of Tanzimar reforms) must be pointed out, the approach of confessionalization should be connected with the topic of the power networks constructed inside and outside of the Empire. See among others Tijana Krstić, "Illuminated by the

This analysis allows an interpretation that correctly aims to highlight the historical value of the Ottoman past: to see the emergence of national movements in the Balkans, and by extension the uprisings that aspired to revolution, as neither autonomous awakenings nor as the result of Great Power competition in the eastern Mediterranean[20] but as corresponding to the revolutionary process that marked the history of the West. The nationalist movements in eastern and southeastern Europe, an area extending from Poland to Greece, continuously negotiate their identities according to the West's internal fragmentations. More specifically, we could describe the Balkan national movements from their inception as the ripple effect from the revolutions in the West, especially those taking place in Paris.

Light of Islam and the Glory of the Ottoman Sultanate—Self-Narratives of Conversion to Islam in the Age of Confessionalization", *Comparative Studies in Society and History* 51:1, 2009, pp. 35–63, Nathalie Clayer, "The dimension of confessionalisation in the Ottoman Balkans at the time of Nationalisms", in H. Grandits, N. Clayer and R. Pichler, *Conflicting Loyalties in the Balkans. The Great Powers, the Ottoman Empire, and Nation-Building*, London: I.B. Tauris, 2011, pp. 89–109.

[20] An early attempt to solve this problem could be traced in the work of Dimitrije Djordjevic and Stephen Fischer-Galati, *The Balkan Revolutionary Tradition*, New York: Columbia University Press, 1981. For them the roots of the revolutionary tradition in the Balkans should be traced from the moment of the resistance against the Ottoman invasion in fifteenth and sixteenth centuries, although they distinguished the "modern" (merchant- and scholar-dominated) from the pre-modern movements through a classical sociological perspective.

The three and one waves of Balkan nationalism(s)

The essential difference between a revolt and a revolution, except for the existence of a new political horizon which characterizes the latter, is that it can actually only be traced a posteriori.[21] On the other hand, a national movement, although it is signified by processual character, has usually been marked by its revolutionary moment. In this sense, we could separate the Balkan movements into three large categories, according to when they peaked and not necessarily by their supposed beginning or their outcomes. Such a criterion might seem problematic, but it solves two significant problems in the history of the nationalisms of eastern and southeastern Europe. First, it allows us to understand the circumstances under which these uprisings restructured their national past, in other words the way in which they constructed the national symbols that comprised their stereotypes and which mainly created the forms of continuity through national historiographies. And second, we can better understand the way they proposed their establishment as autonomous or independent political entities.

Nevertheless, these three phases of national movements' emergence concern mainly the nineteenth century and should be supplemented with one more definitive moment: the appearance of revolutionary movements in the heart of two important continental empires—the Russian Empire (1905) and the Ottoman Empire (1908).

---

[21] Charles Tilly, *European Revolutions, 1492–1992*, Oxford: Blackwell, 1993.

The case of the Young Turk revolt especially seems like a delayed repercussion of 1848 in the Ottoman lands. But the international reality was different: instead of a peoples' 'spring' in the Ottoman Empire, the nation-states already founded on its old territory would share out its latest acquisitions on the European continent.

And let's begin with this aphorism: all Balkan national revolutions in reality failed militarily but almost always succeeded politically.[22] To explain this contradiction, we need more than a composite of the old historiographical examples in a single one that includes external (Eastern Question) and internal (national movements) factors; we need to understand how these national movements played with the Western world's internal rifts, how they exploited the clashes between the Great Powers, and mainly, how they exploited the defeated colonialists. An exemplary loser was, of course, France: Paris continuously produced revolutions not just because the bourgeoisie had not resolved the problem of its hegemony internally, but because it was being defeated by the English in North America and the Germans in the heart of Europe.

As implied at the start of this essay, it is arguable that the Greek and Serbian revolts could be seen as resulting from the upheavals created by the 1789 Revolution and the Napoleonic Wars which followed.[23] Indeed, in the

---

[22] See also Mazower, *The Balkans*, p. 92, a similar estimation limited on the development of the Greek and Serbian revolutions.

[23] For a thorough historiographical survey of the revolts in the premodern Balkans, see Olga Katsiardi-Hering, "Von den Aufständen zu den Revolutionen christilicher Untertanen des Osmanischen Reiches in Südosteuropa (ca. 1530–1821). Ein Typologisierungsversuch", *Südost-Forschungen*, 68, 2009, pp. 96–137. The link which connected the most influential revolutions of the nineteenth-century Balkans, the

Greek case, it is interesting that the Greek revolution is described as a War of Independence—with each of these terms corresponding to different interpretations.[24] To a certain extent, one uprising triggered the other: beyond the revolts of 1807–1808 in the Greek lands, discussed earlier, Ypsilantis's lieutenant, Georgakis Olympios, had fought alongside Obrenović, while the first brothers whom Ypsilantis appeals to in his famed proclamation to fight "for faith and country" (Υπέρ Πίστεως και Πατρίδος) are the Serbs.

In one of his most significant contributions to modern Greek history, Gunnar Hering comments on a paper by Vassilis Kremmydas about whether we can apply Crane Brinton's theory of rising expectations in the Greek case.[25] According to this theory, revolutions occur when

---

Serbian and the Greek, are the revolts of the Peloponnese and Thessaly around 1808, and their importance must be featured by the relative historiography.

[24] See for example the title of the classical monograph of Douglas Dakin (*The Greek struggle for independence, 1821–1833*, Berkeley: University of California Press, 1973) but also the last book of Thomas Gallant (*The Edinburgh History of the Greeks, 1768 to 1913: The Long Nineteenth Century*, Edinburgh: Edinburgh University Press, 2015). In his third chapter (pp. 51–106) which has been entitled "The War that changed the Greek World" Gallant uses alternatively the terms of "revolution" and "revolt", but seems to finally choose the "War of Independence" as his basic historiographical reference.

[25] Gunnar Hering, "Zum Problem der Ursachen revulutionärer Erhebungen am Anfang des 19. Jahrhunderts", in Choliolcev-Mack-Suppan, *Nationalrevolutionäre Bewegungen in Südosteuropa im 19. Jh.* Vienna 1992, pp. 17–30. The article of Vasillis Kremmydas first appeared in 1976 as "Η οικονομική κρίση στον ελλαδικό χώρο στις αρχές του 19ου αιώνα και οι Επιπτώσεις της στην Επανάσταση του 1821" [*Economic Crisis in the Greek Lands at the beginning of the 19th Century and its Consequences on the Revolution of 1821*], *Mnimon* 6 (1976) 16–33. Kremmydas returned with a second article trying to support his thesis from the critics although he did not cite Hering's article, in "Προεπαναστατική κρίση: η οικονομική κρίση και η πορεία προς το Εικοσιένα" [*Pre-revolutionary Cri-*

an extended period of economic growth is violently disrupted by an acute economic crisis. In the Greek case, this huge economic growth is marked by Catherine the Great's Russo-Turkish wars which not only benefitted the Greek diaspora communities (chiefly, those in the Danubian Principalities), but also the growth of "native" bourgeois elements, in particular the shipping capital of the Aegean and Ionian Islands as the Treaty of Küçük Kaynarca facilitated trade in the eastern Mediterranean. The Napoleonic Wars were the apogee of this growth process, when shipowners' profits multiplied as a result of the British fleet's blockade of the French ports. Breaking the embargo was hugely profitable. However, the end of the Napoleonic Wars in 1815 broke the economic chain linking the shipowner-trader to the monoculture farmers of the Peloponnese, usually through the intermediary Peloponnese oligarchy of 'elders' (*prokritoi*)—a rupture that served to radicalize all the links in this chain.

Hering observed that this theory could also easily be applied to the Serbian case. Here, economic growth was a slow process that followed in the wake of the stabilization of the Austrian-Ottoman border after 1739. Certainly, it did not produce a strong diaspora bourgeoisie as in the Greek case, but it did help foster the emergence of a strong merchant class that exploited Austrian imperial privilege in the Serbian community on the other side of the border. Nonetheless, the rise of Selim III and his fateful decision to allow large numbers of Janissaries at the Belgrade paşalık in 1793 and, of even greater significance, the upheavals wrought by the Napoleonic Wars

sis: The Economic Crisis and the Route to 1821], *Mnimon* 24, 2002, pp. 71–84.

naturally led, in a manner of speaking, to the 1804 Serbian uprising. But he noted that the theory overly emphasized economics to be able to include the cultural processes that lead to a revolutionary rupture. Indeed, we would say that a comparison of these two revolutionary movements would be interesting, not only for the economic and social backdrops, but also for the outcome in terms of the formation of political power. Both stemmed from the Napoleonic Wars, and in both cases the solution was offered almost simultaneously with the 1829 Treaty of Adrianople. In the Greek case, the establishment of an independent state is effectively supported by the critical balance of power between England and Russia as to which of these Great Powers would control the newly formed state. In the Serbian case, we would say that the balance is maintained mainly between Austria and Russia. For the first time in the Balkans, at the two ends, northern and southern, states are created through failed military revolts that nonetheless activate rifts on the European political stage. There are two prerequisites: not just the defeat of the revolutionaries in Paris, but also, following the ascent of Nicholas I, the turn of Russian policy towards the protection of Orthodox populations of the Ottoman Empire, as recorded in the treaties of Küçük Kaynarca in 1774 and Jassy in 1792. In spite of all this, in these cases the issue of establishing political power was resolved in different ways. In the Serbian instance, despite Obrenović's defeat of Karađorđe in 1817, it allowed these military leaders to simultaneously emerge as political leaders. Conversely, in the Greek case, the civil wars prevented the conversion of the military leader, Kolokotronis, into a political leader, as it also prevented the political leader Kapodistrias's transformation into a sovereign. The complex political balance between social groups with divergent political orientations—*kodjabashis* or primates, *klephts* or brigands, ship owners, members of the Phanariot world as well as representatives of the Greek "diaspora"—render the formation of Greek political hegemony more fragile. However, both Greeks and Serbs traversed their revolutionary course at a particularly crucial transitional phase of ideological processing in Europe, when the Enlightenment paradigm was on the wane and was gradually being replaced by the Romantic perception of Nation. The fact that both will soon restructure their separatist and thus anti-imperialist ideology with *Megali Idea*/Načertanije theories, which they will express that same year, 1844, illustrates their rapid adaption to the new conditions.

It was logical that the second wave of national movements in the Balkans would be determined by the establishment of the (independent) Greek and the (autonomous) Serbian nation-states, but it was further accelerated by the 1830 and the 1848 Paris Revolutions. Both of them certainly did not create these movements, but they finalized their structure and their basic orientation.

The 1848 revolution in Paris rippled through other European cities very quickly and set off revolts with liberal demands for reform and national independence. Soon afterwards, the Habsburgs' empire was called on to manage unrest in Hungary. In 1848, in Budapest, the Hungarian nationalist Lajos Kossuth demanded a Hungarian Constitution. Actually, it was not the first time the Hungarians and especially the aristocracy had claimed autonomy rights: but for the first time the Hungarian national movement was synchronized by the claims of the other nationalities of the empire which tried to undermine the Hungarian primacy. Kossuth's positions spread throughout the empire, fostering an uprising of all social classes against Habsburg autocracy with demands for administrative and economic reforms. The government's rejection of these demands led to the first upheavals in Vienna. Ferdinand decided to scuttle Metternich, who was identified with the authoritarian empire, to restore calm. But this gesture only encouraged the rebels to press their demands for reform and national indepen-dence. The emperor granted the Magyars' demands for political rights, a free press, religious tolerance, and abolition of imperial privileges, and gave them their own government departments. In other words, he allowed them some autonomy within the empire. But the nationalist Kossuth's declaration of Hungarian as the official language of the state led to a civil war with Hungary's minorities—Croats, Serbs, Slovaks, Romanians, Ukrainians and Germans. The Croats were bothered most as they enjoyed certain privileges under the Habsburgs. The civil war that erupted between the Croats and Magyars was to Ferdinand's benefit as it allowed him to wipe out the rebel movement with the help of Croatian and Russian troops.

The Czechs followed the Hungarian example, led by František Palacký, demanding the union of Bohemia, Moravia, and Silesia into a single administrative entity with its own Diet and ministry. The Czechs also demanded that their language be considered equal to German in education and administrative issues. However, the political freedoms that had been granted were either abolished or curtailed as a result of clashes between Czechs and Germans.

In Austria, where Metternich's sacking had fomented tension, the situation was eased by a commitment to abolish the peasants' obligations to the feudal lords. But the liberal revolt was gradually led to failure. The rebels saw their freedoms and rights restricted. This led to new unrest and clashes in Vienna in October of 1848, which were put down by General Alfred Windisch-Grätz. Ferdinand resigned and was succeeded by Franz Joseph, who sought Russian help to crush the uprising in Budapest and succeeded in putting down the Magyars and Hungary; he also rescinded the reforms agreed by Ferdinand. There were also uprisings in Poland, where the cities sought to shed Prussian and Russian control.[26]

The Bulgarian, Romanian, and Croatian national movements are seen emerging between the 1830 and 1848 revolutions. For the Romanians, Moldavians, and Vlachs, the 1848 Revolution was in fact the only one in which they participated, if one considers that the Organic laws of Moldavia and Wallachia resulted from a Russian occupation in the 1830s. For the Croats, participation in the suppression of the Hungarian national movement reaffirmed their position within the Habsburg Empire. Finally, for the Bulgarians, we would say that 1848 marked the end of their delusions: that is, the view that they could develop some noteworthy military movements with separatist ambitions in Constantinople's front yard. It is that critical moment when Stefan Vogoridi's position as the Ottoman Empire's surrogate in Moldavia is destabilized and the moment when, in the wake of Neofit Božveli's failure to be elected bishop of

---

[26] Ian Armour, *A History of Eastern Europe, 1740-1918: Empires, Nations and Modernization*, New York: Bloomsbury Academic, 2012.

Veliko Tărnovo, the Bulgarian nationalists made the big decision to move their political battle into the heart of the empire, to Istanbul. For the first time, a national movement in the Empire raised the issue of separation from the religiously defined millet to which it belonged and from the ruling church, the Ecumenical Patriarchate, but not from the Ottoman state. Nonetheless, it could be argued that this Bulgarian quirk characterizes all three movements in the second wave. In all three cases, the nationalists' goal was not just the separation and clash with the political ruler—the Ottoman or the Habsburg—but also with the cultural ruler—the Greek or the Hungarian. This is quite clear in the Bulgarian case, but also occurred in the Romanian, where the power of the land-owning boyars was re-established on an anti-Phanariot basis, just as in the case of the Croats who saw a greater threat in the Hungarians' attempt to impose their language on them than in any Viennese absolutism.

In assuming the task of sharing out political power between conservatives and liberals, the Romanian boyars had to do so largely by delegitimizing the Phanariot period before 1821. For example, Mihail Kogălniceanu, one of the most influential Romanian statesmen and intellectuals, observes:

> Such a book [about the History of the Romanian People] should be for us what The Iliad was to the Greeks. And believe me, gentlemen, that your history has events, persons, that are not lacking in comparison to the ancient heroes if one removed the poetic aura which sanitised them. Everything stems from the fact that the heroic and mythological eras have long passed and that today we no longer find poetry even in the verses of the poets and that there was only one Homer in the world.

Clearly, the history of Sparta, Athens, Rome, is more interesting than ours to a foreigner—on one hand because the Greeks and Romans are peoples who summarise ancient civilization and, on the other, because their influence is preserved today through religion, science, the arts, and the land we inherited from them and, finally, because all of our youth's Classical education is founded in the history of the Greeks and the Romans. But chiefly because the actions of these peoples were recorded by men like Thucydides, Tacitus, Titus Livius. In this respect, I myself recognise the international interest in Greek and Roman history, but with respect to individual courage, the bravery of the acts, the steadfast defense, the generosity and the valor of our Voivode who, in a small tent and with few means, made enormous achievements and, in all these, gentlemen, I'm not afraid to say that our history does not lack anything compared to the history of any other people, old or new.[27]

Thus the Romantic characteristics that many scholars have identified in these three national movements are just one side of the issue. The other is an elusive realization when it comes to the two empires that dominated in the Balkans: that the Ottomans and Habsburgs effectively imposed their dominance for a considerable stretch of the long nineteenth century with privileged alliances, the former with the Greeks and the latter with the Hungarians. Thus the suggestion made in 1876 by Georgios Zarifis, a prominent Constantinople banker, to the English embassy that the Ottoman Empire be united with

---

[27] Mihail Kogălniceanu, Inaugural Speech for the course of the National History in *Academia Mihăileană*, 24 November 1843, in *1848 La Români o Istorie in Date și Mărturii* [*1848 in Romanians or History in Documents and Testimonies*], vol. I, Bucarest: Editura Științifică și Enciclopedică 1982, 212–213.

the Greek kingdom along the lines of the Austro-Hungarian *Ausgleich* is not random at all.

But just as it is interesting to compare the two national movements of the first wave, for the reasons mentioned earlier, it would also be interesting to compare the Greek (culturally dominant) movement with perhaps its most important (subjugated) rival of the mid-nineteenth century.

The comparison of the Greek and Bulgarian national movements that converged on the same goal—rupture from the Ottoman Empire—would obviously result in identifying similarities between them. The fact that they emerged and grew at different points of the nineteenth century could be a springboard for examining their differences. Nonetheless, this unity of space which gives rise to some of their similarities and the difference in their timeframe that generates dissimilarities deserve more careful analysis, especially for one reason: these two movements were not just against the Ottoman Empire but also faced off against each other by claiming more or less the same territories in the central Balkan space, particularly from the moment they took shape as state entities.

The Greek Revolution—like the Serbian one—resulted from complex processes but to a significant degree was also the result of upheavals created by the Napoleonic Wars in an Ottoman Empire that had already entered a state of extended crisis. The fact that the revolution prevailed in central Greece, the Peloponnese, and the Aegean islands should not be cause for us to overlook the fact that the earlier revolutionary plans of Rigas and his comrades, as well as those of the Philike Etaireia, had hoped to spread the revolution through the

Ottoman Empire (or at least throughout its European territory), and called on all peoples to join it.[28] Despite the obvious influence of the principles of the French Revolution on these revolutionary plans, the prospect of the empire's dissolution and transformation into a strong bourgeois state, with Constantinople as the capital, was equally evident.

Of course, these delusions were not shared by the Bulgarian national movement. The late nineteenth century had shown that it would be very difficult for the Ottoman Empire to maintain its unity. The Bulgarian movement was not just against the Ottoman Empire's unity but also (and mainly) against Greek cultural dominance as expressed partly through the Ecumenical Patriarchate but chiefly through the Greek-speaking Orthodox urban class that managed to dominate the Balkans in the wake of the eighteenth-century Russo-Ottoman wars.

We have at our disposal a basic model for comparing national movements: Miroslav Hroch's model.[29] This is an evolutionary model based on the growth of every national movement in three phases. In the first, a group of intellectuals manages the problem of national identity; in the second, the issue of national identity becomes the subject of concern for the broader masses, mainly the middle classes and the bourgeoisie; in the third, it emerges as a mass movement that often resorts to an armed uprising.

---

[28] Indeed, Rigas's call to arms in *Thourios* even addressed the Turks oppressed by the Ottoman regime.

[29] Miroslav Hroch, *Social Preconditions of National Revival in Europe: A Comparative Analysis of the Social Composition of Patriotic Groups among the Smaller European Nations*, Cambridge, Cambridgeshire; New York: Cambridge University Press, 1985.

If we follow the evolutionary course suggested by Hroch, we can lay some foundations for making comparisons, although we can also see some diversions from the model that arise mainly from the peculiarities of the Ottoman Empire as compared to the Habsburg Empire.[30] With regards to the first phase, in both cases we have comparable intellectual phenomena, movements of intellectuals who have shaped a definition of national identity. On the one hand, we have what K. T. Dimaras called Modern Greek Enlightenment and on the other we have Bulgarian renaissance, or *Vazrâzdane*. Indeed, the similarities go further: both phenomena emerge in roughly the same period—in 1762, Paisii Hilandarski writes his famous *Slavo-Bulgarian History* and in 1766, Evgenios Voulgaris translates Locke's Essay into Greek. Both are clerics who abandon the ideological world dominated by the church to join secular modernity. Nonetheless, the phenomenon of Modern Greek Enlightenment peaks in the forty-year period spanning 1770 to 1821, culminating with the eruption of the independence revolt. Conversely, Paisii Hilandarski and Sofronii Vračanski appear to be the forefathers of a long intellectual process that blossoms from the 1840s onwards.

This means that what Hroch describes as the first phase, in the Bulgarian case corresponds to reality both in terms of reinforcing the urban classes and the first attempted armed uprisings in the 1840s. More so, the Bulgarian national movement develops in a period where, at the European level, the ideas of the Enlight-

---

[30] Miroslav Hroch, "Is there a Southeast European Type of Nation-Formation?", in Dimitris Stamatopoulos, *Balkan Nationalism(s) and the Ottoman Empire*, vol.3, Istanbul: Isis Press, vol I, pp. 13–27.

enment recede as the ideas of political Romanticism gain traction. In many representatives of this period, from the conservative Gavril Krâstević to the radical Georgi Rakovski, one sees a combination of Enlightenment and Romantic elements, which is only natural as they must respond both to the Romantic *Megali Idea* of the Greeks and the Serbs' *Načertaniye*. To take two intellectuals who lived most of their lives in Paris as two similar examples for comparison: Adamantios Korais, who was chiefly responsible for introducing the ideas of European Enlightenment at the turn of the 18th to the 19th century, and Petar Beron, with his famous primer.[31] Versed in the Hegelian philosophical process, Beron tried to construct something similar, which he called *Panépistème* and in which the "theoretical" and the "empirical" comprised a single whole. This was essentially a Romantic endeavor. As Atanas Stamatov correctly observes, at the moment when post-Hegelian philosophical thought in Europe was abandoning its effort to erect holistic philosophical frameworks, Beron was doing the opposite in the "European periphery" (even though he had spent the 1840s working in Paris).[32] The Bulgarian uprising stems primarily from the Romantic environment that took shape in Europe after the 1848 uprising. To be precise, we are dealing with a Romanticism of the periphery rather than the European center, but since it was directed against the integrity of a despotic empire, it also drew on the ideological armory of the European Enlightenment.

---

[31] Petâr Beron, *Origine de l'unique couple humain, dispersion de ses descendants*, vol. 7, Paris, 1864.

[32] Atanas Stamatov, "Paradoxes in the Bulgarian Reception of European Philosophical Thought", *Studies in East European Thought*, 53, 2001, p. 6–7.

With regards to the second phase, that is, the spread of the concept of national identity taking shape among the middle classes, we can, of course, find some basic similarities between the two movements. In the Greek case, the idea spread mainly to the urban classes of the diaspora, to the bourgeois Greek communities of central Europe, the Danubian Principalities, Russia, and the eastern Mediterranean. In the Bulgarian case, similar communities were created by the Bulgarians, especially after the 1828–9 war, in the Romanian and Crimean cities. Nonetheless, in both cases—but especially the Bulgarian—there is a question as to how to verify the "internal" urbanization of the national space. The Greek elders of the Peloponnese and most of the shipowners of the islands certainly practiced a significant bourgeois merchant activity, but so did the corbaci and the abaci of the Bulgarian hinterland. However, what is certain is that in the central Balkan space, bourgeois activity in the large urban centers was facilitated by the Greek and Vlach element while, conversely, the agricultural interior was dominated by Slavophone populations. Certainly, the founder of the first Bulgarian school, Vasil Aprilov, could be considered bourgeois in the broader sense of the word.

Perhaps the most critical phase in the Hroch model is the third, that is, the phase when the national movement acquires its mass character and armed expression. The Greek Revolution of 1821 and the April 1876 Bulgarian up-rising have a basic similarity: they were suppressed, almost completely, by the Egyptian and Ottoman military forces. There is another similarity: they prompted external military interventions—the Battle of Navarino and the Russo-Ottoman War of 1828–9 in the one case and the Russian invasion of 1877 and the Bulgarian liberation through the Treaty of San Stefano in the other. Nonetheless, there is a significant difference, and this is precisely in the different meanings of the words "revolution" and "uprising." The distinction has to do with the length of the armed conflict but more so with the expression of a program of state and social reform that leads to the establishment of a civil state. In reality, this program is not the result of plans that precede the revolution: which is what makes the difference. That is, in the Greek case, it is not the revolutionary strategies laid by Rigas or the Philike Etaireia but on the contrary, the problem of power as outlined during the revolution—and not solely the Constitutions of the Greek Revolution, which are known for their liberal character, but also the clashes within the revolution that highlighted, in an urgent manner, the issue of leadership among the various social groups. Conversely, in the Bulgarian case, this problem of power was settled by the National Assembly of Veliko Târnovo in 1879 and not by the April uprising, which had been preceded by the confrontation between Bulgarian conservatives and liberals in Istanbul. This is pre-cisely why Vasil Levski's contribution is important.

As we know, Levski participated in all Bulgarian attacks on the Ottoman Empire between 1862 and 1868. Already, at the end of the 1860s, he had developed a revolutionary theory that was a decisive step towards a Bulgarian liberation movement. This theory (which reflected the ideas of his spiritual mentor Karavelov) saw liberation as an armed Bulgarian uprising against the Ottoman Empire. The uprising had to be prepared, controlled, and coordinated by a central revolutionary organization. This organization would include local revolutionary committees across Bulgaria and organize a network of revolutionaries beyond the influence of any external power. Levski's theory stemmed from the repeated failures to realize Rakovski's ideas, that is, to provoke an armed uprising through the activity of armed groups, or *cheti*, from neighboring countries. Levski also outlined the future form of government of a liberated Bulgaria: a popular democracy, which he described as a pure and sacred democracy, inspired by the French Revolution's Declaration of the Man and of the Citizen.

We could thus say that the Bulgarian national movement finds its own Rigas in Levski—and quite possibly also its Athanasios Diakos, as we know Levski had been ordained in his youth. However, while Levski is the vital link for the April uprising, we cannot say that the entire Bulgarian national movement aimed at defecting from the Ecumenical Patriarchate's control. Stoyan Čomakov, the leader of the Bulgarian radicals in Istanbul, is a typical case. Čomakov had reservations about the Russian military intervention, favoring the solution of the Ottoman-Bulgarian co-existence in the imperial context like the elite of the Greek Orthodox community of this time—a stance one would have expected from his conservative rivals such as Krâstević or Marko Balabanov.

And this is the point where Hroch's model perhaps needs to be "broadened." Bulgarians and Greeks (like Serbs, Orthodox Albanians, Moldavians and Wallachians) are not solely under the authority of the Ottoman state but simultaneously belong to the Rum millet. The demand had been made very early—indeed, since Paisii—and led to the Bulgarians' distancing from Greek cultural dominance. The national movements of the Balkan peoples while in the Ottoman Empire's sphere of influence was also against the Hellenization processes (recall the examples of the Bulgarians, Romanians, and Albanians), while in the Austro-Hungarian Empire's sphere of influence was also against the processes of Magyarization. In other words, in both cases, it was also against the imperial power's privileged ally. What is worth noting, however, is that after the 1821 Revolution, the empire's Romioi gradually lost the privileged position of the Phanariot period, while persons of Bulgarian descent such as Stefan Vogoridi participated in the Patriarchate's administration and acquired strong footholds in Ottoman power.[33] This means that the clash over the issue of cultural dominance was not conducted on the terms Paisii discerned in the late eighteenth century but clearly on more advantageous ones for the issue of the Bulgarian Renaissance. Of course, as in the 1844 confrontation over the issue of who would become Metropolitan of Veliko Târnovo, Istanbul's conservatives showed a preference for someone loyal to Ottoman power and the Patriarchate like Neophytos Vyzantios and not a radical nationalist like Neofit Božveli.

Another point we must examine critically in Hroch's model is its evolutionary character. Especially in the Bulgarian case, we see that the three phases are intertwined and there is no clear delineation and no smooth passage from one to the other.

---

[33] Dimitris Stamatopoulos, "Bulgarian Patriarchs and Bulgarian Neophanariotes: Continuities and Discontinuities in the Ecumenical Patriarchate during the Age of Revolution", in Michel De Dobbeleer, Stijn Vervaet, *(Mis)understanding the Balkans. Essays in Honor of Raymond Detrez*, Ghent: Academia Press 2013, pp. 45–57.

However, it is certain that in both cases, Greek and Bulgarian, we are looking at national secessionist movements (which Hans Kohn categorizes as "East European" and Anthony Smith as "ethnic" nationalisms), which contributed to a despotic empire's collapse. Both were inspired by the French Revolution's democratic ideals but generated intensely centralized states with kings imposed by foreign powers—something which no doubt would have made Levski despondent had he survived the uprising. And, both were touched off by the French Enlightenment but ended up defining national identity according to German Romanticism. Certainly both were a definitive moment in the democratization of the societies in southeastern Europe.

Finally, the events of 1871, and their consequences (the Eastern Crisis, and so on) conclude the process of each movement's national completion and set off a third wave of nationalism with the final establishment of the nation-states of the three former national movements as well as the emergence of an Albanian[34] and a Slav-Macedonian[35] national movement. The former were completed with the end of the Balkan Wars, while the latter remained unresolved until the end of the Second World War. These two national movements could be seen as the failure of earlier ones to complete their homogenizing—in the Albanian instance—or irredentist—in the Slavo-Macedonian case—aims. The Albanian national movement emerges from the wreckage of Otto-

---

[34] George W. Gawrych, *The Crescent and the Eagle: Ottoman Rule, Islam and the Albanians, 1874–1913*, London; New York: I.B. Tauris, 2006.
[35] Vemund Aarbakke, *Ethnic Rivalry and the Quest for Macedonia, 1870–1913*, Boulder, Colorado: East European Monographs; New York: Distributed by Columbia University Press, 2003

manism[36] in the transition from the Ottoman imperial ideology to Pan-Islamism[37], while the Slav-Macedonian movement emerged from the clash between Serbs and Bulgarians, mainly, over this Slav-speaking population magma in the Macedonian plains in the wake of the failure of the San Stefano Treaty.[38]

---

[36] See for example the case of Sami Frasheri or Semseddin Sami, Ömer Faruk Akün, "Semseddin Sami", *Islam Ansiklopedisi*, vol. 11, Eskisehir: Anadolu Üniversitesi Güzel Sanatlar Fakültesi, 1997 [1967], pp. 411–422, chiefly pp. 415–416. Sami accused Greek nationalism of expanding its leagues throughout the empire in support of its irredentist aims rather than to contribute to the education process. He also charged that the use of the term "Rumeli" was a deliberate attempt to confuse the words "Rum" and "Greek" and the latter's secessionist visions. This criticism in the late 1870s against all unstated goals of Greek nationalism lay the ground for Sami's complete about-face on the ideas of an emerging Albanian nationalism in the framework of the Hamidian pan-Slavic policy. But the issue of abandoning the principles of the Islamic Ummah was even more complicated for a Bektaşi nationalist.

[37] On Pan-Islamism as the Ottoman state's dominant ideology during the reign of Abdul Hamid, see Azmi Özcan, *Pan-Islamism: Indian Muslims, the Ottomans and Britain, 1877–1924*, Leiden-New York: Brill, 1997; Jacob M. Landau, *The Politics of Pan-Islamism: Ideology and Organization*, Oxford, England: Clarendon Press; New York: Oxford University Press, 1990; Selim Deringil, *The Well-Protected Domains: Ideology and Legitimization of Power in the Ottoman Empire, 1876–1909*, London; New York: I.B. Tauris; (in the U.S.A. and in Canada distributed by St. Martin's Press), 1998, Kemal Karpat, *The Politicization of Islam: Reconstructing Identity, State, Faith, and Community in the Late Ottoman State*, New York: Oxford University Press, 2001. On the positive way in which the Hamidian state handled the "Albanian nation" (*Arnavut milleti*) as a fundamental part of imperial policy in the Balkans, see Savfet Pasa's 1880 memorandum as presented by Nathalie Clayer in *Aux origines du nationalisme albanais. La naissance d'une nation majoritairement musulmane en Europe*, Paris: Karthala, 2007, pp. 262–263.

[38] See, for example, Krste Misirkov, *Za makedonckite raboti* [*On Macedonian Matters*], Sofia, 1903, in which he deems it necessary for the Macedonians to distance themselves from every form of foreign propaganda, resist the proselytising efforts of Bulgarian, Serbian and Greek intellectuals and follow a common religious and national direction. In any case, secession from Bulgaria would not be painful as, according to

Approaching Balkan revolutionary movements as the result of ruptures sustained by the Great Powers, either internally (revolutions) or externally (wars), would allow us to take the long view of this process so that the inversion of events from the start of the nineteenth century at its end do not seem coincidental.

But let us re-examine the case of the Christian-Muslim agreement of 1808 in the Peloponnese described at the beginning of this essay under the light of the previous analysis. It is unlikely that the Muslim side (the Muslim notables of the Peloponnese) had suggested this model of egalitarianism, and it is very unlikely that the Christian side, even if it suggested it, actually meant it. We can, however, be sure that the ideological background was definitely given by French policy. Remember that the co-existence of Christians and Muslims was one of the main motifs of the policy followed by Napoleon in Egypt.

Napoleon in his famous decree to the Egyptian people issued in Alexandria in 1798 included the following:

> Cheikhs, cadis, imams, chorbadjis et notables de la nation, dites au peuple que nous sommes les vrais amis des musulmans. La preuve en est que nous sommes allés à Rome et avons renversé le gouvernement du pape, qui poussait toujours les chrétiens à faire la guerre aux musulmans. Nous avons ensuite été à Malte et avons détruit les chevaliers qui prétendaient que Dieu leur ordonnait de faire la guerre aux musulmans.

Misirkov, the interests and needs of the two people had already been delineated 25 years earlier and "the present situation is simply the product of compromise"—it is the chronological distancing from the Treaty of San Stefano to the Ilinden uprising.

> De tout temps, les Français sont les vrais amis du sultan ottoman
> (que Dieu éternise son empire !) et les ennemis de ses ennemis. Les
> mamelouks au contraire ne sont point soumis au Sultan et se sont ré-
> voltés contre son autorité. Ils ne suivent que leurs caprices.[39]

This reduction of differences between Christians and Muslims as well as the defense of the Ottoman legitimacy while catalyzing it at the same time, are reminiscent of and perhaps heralded the approach that would be followed by the Serbian (1804) and Greek (1808) insurgents a few years later.

What is significant for the argument set out in this essay is that, from the outset, this process of successive uprisings in the Balkans—many of which were only subsequently viewed as revolts—is not only associated with the political-military events that triggered the revolutions in the West, but also with a clear ideological influence, a repetition of the motifs of what we might call imperial nationalism that transcends the argument of a code of values regarding equality and freedom. Recall, for example, the special relationship we must discern between the final coalescing of the Greek 'Megali Idea' and the ideology of France's Second Empire,[40] the corresponding

---

[39] https://fr.wikisource.org/wiki/Déclaration_du_général_Bonaparte_au_peuple_égyptien (25.07.2018), s. also The National Archives, London FO78/19, pp. 265-266.

[40] If 1848 was, for obvious reasons, the turning point, then the establishment of the Second Empire in 1851–1852 touches off a series of discourses about the East, which, activated by the Crimean War as well as the "cultural imperialism" exercised in its wake by Napoleon III, redefined the relations between Catholic France and the nations and religions of the Ottoman Empire. The issue of the French intervention in the Ottoman East must be related to the formulation and transformation of the Great Idea from its cultural to its irredentist version. It has been correctly suggested that the shaping of the Great

French influence on the unique Latinism of nineteenth-century Romanian intellectuals,[41] the correlation of Albanian nationalism's ideals during its early stages with Abdul Hamid's Pan-Islamism,[42] or even the closeness of the 'crossroads of civilizations' motifs that all Balkans use with the Euro-Asian theories developed in nineteenth-century Russia as an attempt to resolve the problem of national identity as a composite of West and East.[43] If the three waves of national movements can be categorized vertically according to the great internal rifts in the West, then the influence of imperial nationalisms and continental empires of eastern Europe as well as that

---

Idea should be linked to the reform process of the Ottoman Empire; see D. Stamatopoulos, *Byzantium after the Nation: The Problem of the National Continuity in the Balkan Historiographies*, Budapest: CEU Press, 2018 (forthcoming).

[41] Throughout the nineteenth century, Moldo-Wallachian intellectual life had been decisively influenced by "Latinism," the dominant approach to history that had entered the culture through Transylvanian Uniates who studied in Rome. This ideological current ran through the historiographical analyses of the Şcoala Ardeleană's Latinists who, in the late eighteenth century, expressed the view that the inhabitants of Moldavia and Wallachia descended from the Roman conquerors, just like Transylvania's Romanian-speaking populations. Obviously, this required expunging the Dacians from Romanian genealogy. According to this view, the Roman-Dacian wars in the first century resulted in either the Dacian population's destruction or expulsion. See Alex Drace-Francis, *The Making of Modern Romanian Culture: Literacy and the Development of National Identity*, London: I.B. Tauris, 2006, p. 60, and Keith Hitchins, *A Nation Discovered: Romanian Intellectuals in Transylvania and the Idea of Nation 1700–1848*, Bucharest: The Romanian Cultural Foundation Publishing House, 1999, pp. 85–96.

[42] Clayer, *Aux origines du nationalisme albanais*, pp. 272–284.

[43] See also Dimitris Stamatopoulos, "From the Vyzantism of K. Leont'ev to the Vyzantinism of I.I. Sokolov: The Byzantine Orthodox East as a Motif of Russian Orientalism", in Olivier Delouis, Petre Guran (eds.), *Héritages de Byzance en Europe du Sud-Est à l'époque moderne et contemporaine*, Athens: École française d'Athènes 2013, pp. 329–348.

of defeated colonial France in shaping Balkan nationalisms can be the horizontal chain linking them.

Imperial and Balkan nationalism

The clash of imperial discourses merits further theoretical elaboration. The national discourses, even in the late nineteenth century, are defined by or against the imperial framework. The empires of eastern and southeastern Europe within which they developed theoretically belong to the "old model" continental empires in contrast with "modern" colonial/maritime empires of Western Europe; although the emergence of modernity (in practical terms, this is linked to the process of "Westernization" already underway in the Russian, Ottoman, and, of course, Habsburg empires) in the Balkans was already a reality, this does not mean that individual or collective subjects were ready to adapt to or even understand the difference between the organizational structure of a modern type of empire versus the traditional type. Moreover, the distinction between the colonial and continental empires was blurred in the nineteenth century when the Ottoman and especially the Russian empires followed the path of "internal colonization" through the adoption of Western methods of ethnic homogenization—Tanzimat reforms could be considered from this perspective, although the application of the egalitarian reforms did not prevent the crucial peripheries for the Ottoman Empire like Crete, Bosnia or Lebanon from being disturbed by the rise of national or sectarian movements during the last decades of the nineteenth century.[44]

This objective weakness of the subjects to distinguish between new and old imperial forms is very important in terms of how they perceive the restructuring of the procedures for reorganizing the national timeline. National states envisage their present and future on the basis of the imperial model (unaware of the differences between the two types), while empires try to adapt to the new conditions by adopting versions of national organization despite remaining multi-ethnic, multilingual, multifaith, and especially pre-modern in terms of their internal structure. If the Balkan states envisioned their expansion in terms of the imperial paradigm, the empires (Russian and Ottoman), oblivious of their approaching end, understood themselves through the prism of the nation-state. This is a point that deserves further consideration: the appearance of various versions of imperial nationalism in the Eastern empires is irrevocably linked to the problem of their recognition as equals in the eyes of the Western world. The Eastern empires sought recognition and equal status from the West, adopting in reality the orientalist-inspired criteria projected on them: cultural "difference" of which faith comprises the hard core.

---

[44] Here of course we have the question of whether the old (continental) empires of the East encountered in the same way—or better, were influenced in the same way—by the Westernization process. For example, according to Lieven, Russia was already part of the West from the eighteenth century, and it is for just this reason that it does not fall within the model of "continental" empires; rather, it formed a "hybrid" that combined traditional imperial structures and modern forms of colonization in Asia; see Dominic Lieven, "Dilemmas of Empire 1850–1918. Power, Territory, Identity", *Journal of Contemporary History* 34-2, 1999, pp. 163–200.

Precisely at the time when, according to Said, the dominant Orientalist paradigm was consolidated in the West, the Eastern empires responded to Western Orientalism not only by adopting modernizing processes (that is, accepting their systemic inferiority) but also by glorifying that which makes them autonomous and thus culturally equivalent entities, namely religion.[45]

Invoking religion, that is the sole supra-national element that speaks to masses, is not only related to the issue of reconstitution of the legitimizing principle of the Eastern empires in the eyes of its subjects. Naturally, the utility of instrumentalizing faith is obvious in both the case of Hamidian Pan-Islamism[46] as well as in contriving the theory of Russia as the nineteenth century's Third Rome.[47] But predicating imperial nationalism on their cultural/religious "difference" as the central reference, the Eastern empires essentially sought equality and recognition from the West in a manner quite different from that chosen by the Eastern nations during that same period. The nations invoke the scheme of their timeline continuity as the foundation for their claims of space; the empires reflect upon their (religious) ecumenism, a modern ecumenism, precisely to transcend the world's apportionment into nations. The nations seek equality with the West, promoting themselves as "collec-

---

[45] On this, see Stamatopoulos "From the Vyzantism of K. Leont'ev to the Vyzantinism of I.I. Sokolov."

[46] Deringil, *The Well-Protected Domains.*

[47] John Meyendorff, "Was There Ever a 'Third Rome'? Remarks on the Byzantine Legacy in Russia", in: John J. Yannias, *The Byzantine Tradition after the Fall of Constantinople*, Charlottesville Va. and London, 1991, pp. 45–60 and mainly Daniel B. Rowland "Moscow: The Third Rome or the New Israel?," *Russian Review* 55, 1966, pp. 591–614.

tive subjects," the empires as alternative "cultural paradigms."

This contradictory and intertwined ideological movement allows a multitude of intellectuals who are resisting or have yet to adapt to the logic of a nation-state to restructure their will to preserving the empire, focusing mainly on the constitutive element: a different perspective of time from that used by the nation-state.

The long nineteenth century in the Ottoman Balkans ended with a national revolt which, however, this time took place in the heart of the empire, that is, in Istanbul itself. To be exact, Istanbul became subjugated via Thessaloniki in the Young Turk movement which prevailed among the military.

The Young Turk revolution in 1908 undoubtedly marks a milestone in the Ottoman Empire's history, as it was the springboard for Turkish nationalism within its territory and also signaled the beginning of the end of the empire that had dominated the region for roughly seven centuries. Additionally, the repercussions from the Young Turk movement were not confined to the Ottoman Empire's final decade, as its influence extended into the first few decades of the newly-formed Turkish Republic. Thus the political stage of the new nation-state and successor to the Ottoman Empire was dominated by personalities from the Young Turk circle, with Mustafa Kemal Ataturk at the center. Finally, this revolution had an immediate influence on the Greek community inside and outside the Ottoman Empire as, during this period, the dream of the *Megali Idea* was temporarily realized through Greece's annexation of Ottoman territories and, within Greece, through the Goudi military coup d'état in 1909.[48]

The Young Turks' 1908 is directly linked to the Greek officers' 1909. This is not the only time when the history of the Greek state intersects with the history of the Ottoman state in modern times. These intersections proved defining for the clashes, development, but also the end of the *Megali Idea*.

The *Megali Idea* was born in 1844 in the reality that emerged in the wake of the first Tanzimat reforms. The acculturating character it was accorded by then prime minister Ioannis Kolettis in reality meant the alignment of the pro-Western forces in Greece with this modernization experiment.[49] And vice versa: its irredentist character with a rupture in relations between the Greek state and the Ottoman Empire (Crimean War, 1897 War). If 1897 meant the end of the *Megali Idea* in its classic nineteenth-century expression, the confluence of 1908–9 meant its redefinition. But this time it was the empire that showed ambivalence. The Young Turks moved between the principles of old Ottomanism and the hardline nationalists of the Committee for Union and Progress.

On July 7, 1908, the newspaper *Athinai* published a report datelined Constantinople, 6 July:

> This Young Turk movement has a broad character and the Young Turks are trying to sway other peoples of Turkey to join it, especially the Greeks. Yesterday a postal employee was arrested in Peran for

---

[48] Erik J. Zürcher, *The Young Turk Legacy and Nation Building: From the Ottoman Empire to Atatürk's Turkey*, London: I. B. Tauris, 2010.

[49] For the Greek Megali Idea see the classic work of Elli Skopetea, *To 'Protypo Vasileio' kai I megali idea. Opseis tou ethnikou provlimatos stin Ellada (1830–1880)*, [*The Model Kingdom and the Megali Idea. Aspects of the National Question in Greece (1830- 1880)*] Athens: Politypo, 1988.

distributing leaflets inviting Turks and Greeks to shed this unbearable enslavement. What did this leaflet state? 'Turks and Greeks', it said, 'are the better elements of Turkey and we Turks have the right of conquerors but you Greeks are the noble Nation which has the same rights. Cooperation is needed. The foreigners have overrun us. It is only through revolt against the regime that we can rid ourselves of this situation'.

On July 11, 1908, a front-page story in *Athinai* sought to inform readers about the Young Turk movement's background. It is worth noting that the paper invited a Young Turk to author it. The article begins with a passage that outlines the audience's character:

Young Turkism emerges in this period, that is, the idea of creating and reshaping a New Turkey, a New Political Regime, reinforcing Turkey by supporting the course of its populations and rebels with the cooperation of Greeks, Turks, Albanians to defend the East from the cohesion of Constantinople's center of sultans.

The article notes that the Young Turks are neither educated "erudites" nor disenchanted with the Sultan. According to the Young Turks, Young Turkism emerged in 1789 when Turkey understood it was not the Turkey of 1453. The eruption of the French Revolution and the reconstruction of ideas and views regarding the Ottoman Empire, which had already begun to fade and lose power, should be reviewed according to those beliefs and become more liberal based on the Young Turks.

The impetus for founding the movement was provided by the 1807 Treaty of Tilsit. Young Turkism and the idea of shaping a new Turkey and new political regime appear around that time and seem to adopt the French Revolution's views on equality and press freedom. It invited all those within the Ottoman Empire to join, regardless of nationality or religion; it invited everyone to fight and rise up against the East, a sterile regime lacking in freedom and democracy.

The article continues by differentiating between Young Turks and the 'old' Turks:

Old Turks and Young Turks

As a reaction to the Young Turk ideas, the party of the so-called Old Turks (Paleo-Turks) is formed that insists on discriminating between conquerors and conquered, rulers and subjects, rabidly fighting and persecuting the Young Turks by declaring them as anti-Islamic political and state dogmas.

The same article also refers to frequent internal disagreements within the Young Turk movement.

Among the Young Turks there is disagreement, not over ideas but within them. Unable to reach a compromise solution, the Young Turks split into two camps. Those in the Murat camp only accept producing the New Idea; in the opposing camp, they agree on Murat as the unrivalled idea but in collaboration with Abdul Hamid in order to avert internal and external upheavals. This latter camp under Midhat are allied with Abdul Hamid.

Abdul Hamid will be forced by the Young Turks to reintroduce the 1876 Constitution with amendments to Articles 12 and 13 regarding equality of all the citizens, regardless of ethnicity and religion, as well as freedom of the press. However, the Turkish officers' revolution inspired the young Greek officers to take on a similar political initiative. At the same time, especially with the radicalization of their movement following the sultan's coup d'état of 31 March, the Young Turks represented a threat to the Greek state: ambivalence in relation to his prospects had been transferred to Athens. Thus, the Young Turks movement exacerbated the inferiority complex of the Greek army. The combination of all the above led the officers to the conspiracy and the coup which broke out in August 1909.

On May 3rd, the newspaper *Alitheia* (Truth), in its column "Alitheiai" (Truths), the columnist with a historical retrospection links the departure of Sultan Abdul Hamid after the coup by the Young Turks with the removal of King Otto from Greece in 1862. The position of the sultan was taken by the terrorism of the Young Turks, whereas in Greece instead of liberty, the party and courteous absolutism were enthralled, leading the nation to the brink of the cliff. The images of the two states, according to the columnist, are tragically identical, with the only difference that the neighboring state has the hope that the Young Turks seek cooperation with the peoples of the Ottoman Empire in order to achieve calm in the interior. In the Greek case, however, the authoritarian pressure to the detriment of popular interests and the governmental lack of will are intensified. The consequence of these will be, as stated in the article, "the faster eruption of the volcano, whose fumes only the blind do not see."

These quotes reflect very well the expectations and the necessary references and comparisons that the Young Turks Revolution activated in the political imagination of the subjugated peoples of the empire. It appeared that 1908 was a repeat of 1789: the Revolution was a revolution of modernity against the ancient regime of the East. The first act of the drama was played in 1876 and was a defeat for modernists, with the removal of Sultan Murat and the compromise between Midhad Paşa supporters and Abdul Hamid. The Revolution of 1908 was bound to complete the process of modernization that the Eastern crisis had left unresolved. This predominant narrative of the Young Turks naturally took into account the fact that the countries from which this process began, mainly England and France, played a leading role in the economic dependency of the empire. They could not, however, adequately estimate the dynamics of the expansion of the nation-states that circumscribed the empire, especially those who also embraced the promotion of the ideas of modernization/Westernization. During the Balkan wars, Bulgarian nationalism mainly used a crusade of rhetorical discourse: the liberation of Macedonia and Thrace from the Ottomans was a process of Christianization of these areas (mainly by the expulsion or violent Christianization of Muslims, especially Slavs). However, the Greek Great Idea as reformulated by Venizelos had made a remarkable shift in relation to the nineteenth century: if, in the nineteenth century, pro-Western modernizers usually promoted the idea of collaboration with the Ottoman Empire to deal with Slavic threat, Venizelos' modernizing vision was identified with its dissolution, leaving its political opponents, such as Ion Dragoumis, defending ghosts of Helleno-Ottomanism, at a time when it was obvious that they could not be supported by Western powers. For this important change to the Great Idea to have occurred, it was necessary to redefine the goals of Greek nationalism: they were not just irredentist. Moreover, the multi-ethnic environment of Macedonian and Thracian territories no longer allowed this. Venizelos' expansion vision was inspired by the British Empire and Western colonialism. The Greek army would carry the lights on the people of the East: the cultural and the irredentist version of the Great Idea would coincide in a definitive way.

So in some way this movement of modernization from Paris to Istanbul seemed to be the moment when the solution of the "Eastern Question" was identified with the final prevalence of the Balkan nationalisms. However, what actually happened was the failed implementation of colonial methods by a "continental" empire, and their corresponding adoption by the threatening states. If the Ottoman Empire turned out to be the "The Sick Man of Europe," it was because it was unable to turn into a "colonial" empire through a kind of internal colonization, as Russia for example had already done, while at the same time the Greek kingdom—which until then was the other pole of a common anti-Slavist front—was choosing to turn, even though temporarily and eventually failing, into a medium-sized colonial power.

Summary

There are two possible ways of relating the history of the Balkans with the core of developments in Western Europe (and Russia) during the long nineteenth century: by directly linking the revolutionary crises that emerge there with the nationalist uprisings of the Balkan peoples, or by expanding the influence of the main ideological motifs of imperial nationalisms, West and East, on the corresponding Balkan nationalist discourses. This essay argues for combining the two. The first responds to the Orientalist paradigm of the Eastern Question and reminds us that the West was not cohesive internally (or geopolitically or socially or economically). The second reminds us of the nineteenth century's hybridity, something which we should never forget. The fact is that what has been dubbed "the century of nationalisms" is a period during which newly established states imagine themselves as empires, while empires imagine themselves as national states.

Bibliography

Aarbakke, Vemund, *Ethnic Rivalry and the Quest for Macedonia, 1870–1913*, Boulder, Colorado: East European Monographs; New York: Distributed by Columbia University Press, 2003.

Akün, Ömer Faruk, "Semseddin Sami", *Islam Ansiklopedisi*, vol. 11, Eskisehir: Anadolu Üniversitesi Güzel Sanatlar Fakültesi, 1997 [1967], pp. 411–422.

Amantos, Konstantinos, *Οι Βόρειοι γείτονες της Ελλάδας* [*The Northern Neighbours of Greece*], Athens, 1922.

Anscombe, Frederick F., "The Balkan Revolutionary Age", *The Journal of Modern History*, 84:3, September 2012, pp. 572–606.

Armour, Ian, *A History of Eastern Europe, 1740–1918: Empires, Nations and Modernization*, New York: Bloomsbury Academic, 2012.

Augusti, Eliana, *Questioni d'Oriente. Europa e Impero ottomano nel Diritto internazionale dell'Ottocento*, Napoli; Roma: Edizioni scientifiche italiane, 2013.

Bataković, Dušan T., "Balkan-Style French Revolution? The 1804 Serbian Revolution in European Perspective", *Balkanica* XXXVI, 2005.

Beron, Petâr, *Origine de l'unique couple humain, dispersion de ses descendants*, vol. 7, Paris, 1864.

Clayer, Nathalie, *Aux origines du nationalisme albanais. La naissance d'une nation majoritairement musulmane en Europe*, Paris: Karthala, 2007.

Clayer, Nathalie, "The dimension of confessionalisation in the Ottoman Balkans at the time of Nationalisms", in H. Grandits, N. Clayer and R. Pichler, *Conflicting Loyalties in the Balkans. The Great Powers, the Ottoman Empire, and Nation-Building*, London: I.B. Tauris, 2011, pp. 89–109.

Clogg, Richard, *A Concise History of Greece*, Cambridge: Cambridge University Press, 1992.

Dakin, Douglas, *The Greek Struggle for Independence, 1821–1833*, Berkeley: University of California Press, 1973.

Deringil, Selim, *The Well-Protected Domains: Ideology and Legitimization of Power in the Ottoman Empire, 1876–1909*, London; New York: I.B. Tauris. In the U.S.A. and in Canada distributed by St. Martin's Press, 1998.

Djordjevic, Dimitrije and Fischer-Galati, Stephen, *The Balkan Revolutionary Tradition*, New York: Columbia University Press, 1981.

Drace-Francis, Alex, *The Making of Modern Romanian Culture: Literacy and the Development of National Identity*, London: I.B. Tauris, 2006.

Driault, Edouard, *La Question d'Orient depuis ses origines jusqu'a nos jours*, Paris: Félix Alcan, 1898.

Fanon, Frantz, *Les Damnés de la Terre*, Paris: Maspero, 1961.

Frary, Lucien J. and Kozelsky, Mara, *Russian-Ottoman Borderlands: The Eastern Question Reconsidered*, Madison, Wisconsin: The University of Wisconsin Press, 2014.

Gallant, Tom, *The Edinburgh History of the Greeks, 1768 to 1913: The Long Nineteenth Century*, Edinburgh: Edinburgh University Press, 2015.

Gawrych, George W., *The Crescent and the Eagle: Ottoman Rule, Islam and the Albanians, 1874–1913*, London; New York: I.B. Tauris, 2006.

Gradeva, Rossitsa, "Osman Pazvantoğlu of Vidin: Between Old and New", *Princeton Papers: Interdisciplinary Journal of Middle Eastern Studies*, XIII, 2005.

Hayden, Milica Bakić-, "Nesting Orientalisms: The Case of the Former Yugoslavia", *Slavic Review* 54, Winter 1995, p. 917–31.

Hering, Gunnar, *Ökumenisches Patriarchat und europäische Politik, 1620–1638*, Wiesbaden, F. Steiner, 1968.

Hering, Gunnar, "Zum Problem der Ursachen revulutionärer Erhebungen am Anfang des 19. Jahrhunderts", in Choliolcev-Mack-Suppan, *Nationalrevolutinäre Bewegungen in Südosteuropa im 19. Jh.* Vienna 1992, pp. 17–30.

Hitchins, Keith, *A Nation Discovered: Romanian Intellectuals in Transylvania and the Idea of Nation 1700–1848,* Bucharest: The Romanian Cultural Foundation Publishing House, 1999.

Hroch Miroslav, *Preconditions of National Revival in Europe: A Comparative Analysis of the Social Composition of Patriotic Groups among the Smaller European Nations,* Cambridge, Cambridgeshire; New York: Cambridge University Press, 1985.

Hroch, Miroslav, "Is there a Southeast European Type of Nation-Formation?", in Dimitris Stamatopoulos, *Balkan Nationalism(s) and the Ottoman Empire*, vol.3, Istanbul: Isis Press, vol I, 2015, pp. 13–27.

Jelavich, Barbara, *History of the Balkans*, vol.2, Cambridge-New York: Cambridge University Press, 1983.

Karpat Kemal, *The Politicization of Islam: Reconstructing Identity, State, Faith, and Community in the Late Ottoman State*, New York: Oxford University Press, 2001.

Katsiardi-Hering Olga, "Von den Aufständen zu den Revolutionen christilicher Untertanen desosmanisches Reiches in Südosteuropa (ca. 1530–1821). EinTypologisierungsversuch", *Südost-Forschungen*, 68, 2009, pp. 96–137.

Kitromilidis, Paschalis, *Η Γαλλική Επανάσταση και η Νοτιοανατολική Ευρώπη* [*The French Revolution and Southeastern Europe*], Athens: Diatton Publishing House, 1990.

Kogălniceanu, Mihail, Inaugural Speech for the course of the National History in *Academia Mihăileană*, 24 November 1843, in *1848 La Români o Istorie in Date și Mărturii* [*1848 in Romanians or History in Documents and Testimonies*], vol. I, Bucarest: Editura Științifică și Enciclopedică, 1982, pp. 212–213.

61

Kolokotronis, Theodoros, *Διήγησις Συμβάντων της Ελληνικής φυλής από το 1770 έως το 1836*, [Narration of the events of the Greek nation from 1770 to 1836], Athens: H. Nikolaidou Filadelfeos Publications, 1846.

Kremmydas, Vasillis, "Η οικονομική κρίση στον ελλαδικό χώρο στις αρχές του 19ου αιώνα και οι Επιπτώσεις της στην Επανάσταση του 1821" [*Economic Crisis in the Greek Lands at the beginning of the 19th Century and its Consequences on the Revolution of 1821*], *Mnimon* 6, 1976, pp. 16–33.

Kremmydas, Vasillis, "Προεπαναστατική κρίση: η οικονομική κρίση και η πορεία προς το Εικοσιένα" [*Pre-revolutionary Crisis: The Economic Crisis and the Route to 1821*], *Mnimon* 24, 2002, pp. 71–84.

Krstić, Tijana, "Illuminated by the Light of Islam and the Glory of the Ottoman Sultanate—Self-Narratives of Conversion to Islam in the Age of Confessionalization", *Comparative Studies in Society and History* 51:1, 2009, pp. 35–63.

Landau Jacob M., *The Politics of Pan-Islamism: Ideology and Organization*, Oxford, England: Clarendon Press; New York: Oxford University Press, 1990.

Laskaris, Michael Th., *Το Ανατολικόν Ζήτημα 1800-1923 [The Eastern Question 1800-1923]*, vol. 1 (2 parts). Thessaloniki, 1948–1955.

Lieven, Dominic, "Dilemmas of Empire 1850–1918. Power, Territory, Identity", *Journal of Contemporary History* 34-2, 1999, pp. 163–200.

Marriot J. A. R., *The Eastern Question. An Historical Study in European Diplomacy*, Oxford: Clarendon Press, 1918.

Mazower, Mark, *The Balkans: A Short History*, New York: The New Library, 2000.

Meyendorff, John, "Was There Ever a 'Third Rome'? Remarks on the Byzantine Legacy in Russia", in: John J. Yannias, *The Byzantine Tradition after the Fall of Constantinople*, Charlottesville Va. and London, 1991, pp. 45–60.

Miller, William, *The Balkans. Roumania, Bulgaria, Servia, and Montenegro*, New York: G. P. Putnam's sons, 1896.

Misirkov, Krste, *Za makedonckite raboti* [*On Macedonian Matters*], Sofia, 1903.

Özcan Azmi, *Pan-Islamism: Indian Muslims, the Ottomans and Britain, 1877–1924*, Leiden-New York: Brill, 1997.

Rowland, Daniel B., "Moscow: The Third Rome or the New Israel?", *Russian Review* 55, 1966, pp. 591–614.

Skopetea, Elli, *To 'Protypo Vasileio' kai I megali idea. Opseis tou ethnikou provlimatos stin Ellada (1830–1880)*, Athens: Politypo, 1988.

Skopetea Elli, *Η δύση της Ανατολής: εικόνες από το τέλος της Οθωμανικής Αυτοκρατορίας* [*Orient's West: Images of the End of the Ottoman Empire*], Athens, 1992.

Stamatopoulos, Dimitris, *Μεταρρύθμιση και Εκκοσμίκευση: προς μια ανασύνθεση της Ιστορίας του Οικουμενικού Πατριαρχείου τον 19ο αιώνα* [*Reform and Secularization: Towards a Reconstruction of the History of the Ecumenical Patriarchate in the 19th Century*], Athens: Alexandria, 2003.

Stamatopoulos, Dimitris, "Constantinople in the Peloponnese: The Case of the Dragoman of the Morea (Tercüman Bey) Georgios Wallerianos", in A. Anastasopoulos, E. Kolovos (eds.), *Ottoman Rule and the Balkans, 1760–1850*, Rethymnon: University of Crete 2007, 149–164.

Stamatopoulos, Dimitris, "Bulgarian Patriarchs and Bulgarian Neophanariotes: Continuities and Discontinuities in the Ecumenical Patriarchate during the Age of Revolution", in Michel De Dobbeleer, Stijn Vervaet, *(Mis)understanding the Balkans. Essays in Honor of Raymond Detrez*, Ghent: Academia Press 2013, pp. 45–57.

Stamatopoulos, Dimitris, "From the Vyzantism of K. Leont'ev to the Vyzantinism of I.I. Sokolov: The Byzantine Orthodox East as a Motif of Russian Orientalism", in Olivier Delouis, Petre Guran (eds.), *Héritages de*

Byzance en Europe du Sud-Est à l'époque moderne et contemporaine, Athens: École française d'Athènes 2013, pp. 329–348.

Stamatopoulos, Dimitris, *Byzantium after the Nation: The Problem of the National Continuity in the Balkan Historiographies*, Budapest: CEU Press, 2018 (forthcoming).

Stavrianos, Leften Stavros, *The Balkans Since 1453*, New York: Rinehart, 1958.

Tappe, E. D., "The 1821 Revolution in the Romanian Principalities", in R. Clogg (ed.), *The Greek Struggle for Independence*, London: Macmillan 1973, pp. 134–55.

Tilly, Charles, *European Revolutions, 1492–1992*, Oxford: Blackwell, 1993.

Todorova, Maria, *Imagining the Balkans*, Oxford; New York: Oxford University Press, 2009 [¹1997].

Zürcher, Erik J., *The Young Turk Legacy and Nation Building: From the Ottoman Empire to Atatürk's Turkey*, London: I. B. Tauris, 2010.